GREAT MOVIE THEMES

FOR CELLO DUET

arranged by Mr & Mrs Cello

ISBN 978-1-70515-703-9

Cover photo by Kinga Gruszka

Visit Hal Leonard Online at
www.halleonard.com

World headquarters, contact:
Hal Leonard
7777 West Bluemound Road
Milwaukee, WI 53213
Email: info@halleonard.com

In Europe, contact:
Hal Leonard Europe Limited
42 Wigmore Street
Marylebone, London, W1U 2RY
Email: info@halleonardeurope.com

In Australia, contact:
Hal Leonard Australia Pty. Ltd.
4 Lentara Court
Cheltenham, Victoria, 3192 Australia
Email: info@halleonard.com.au

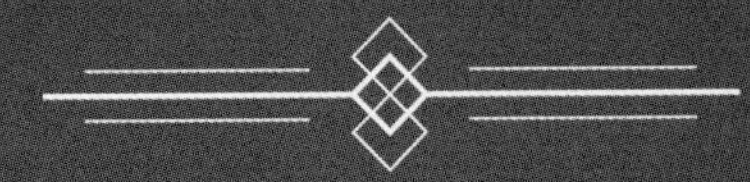

Amarcord

Theme from the film AMARCORD
By Nino Rota
Arranged by Massimiliano Martinelli and Fulvia Mancini

22
mp

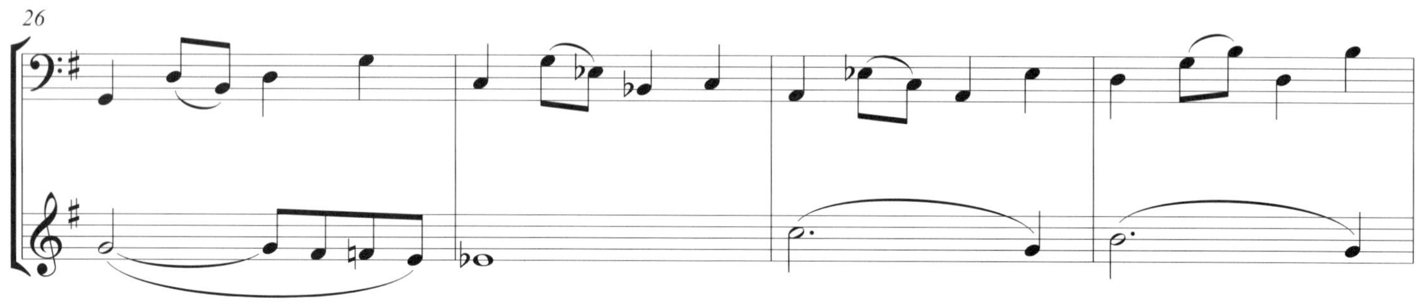
26

30

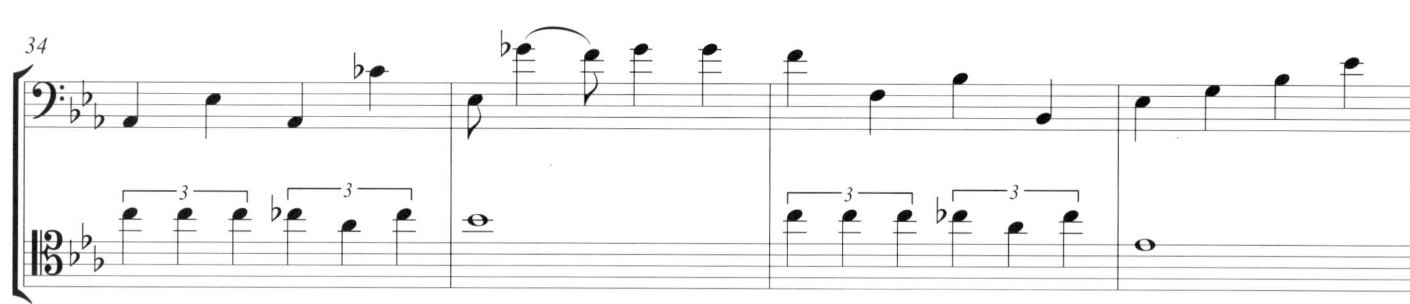
34

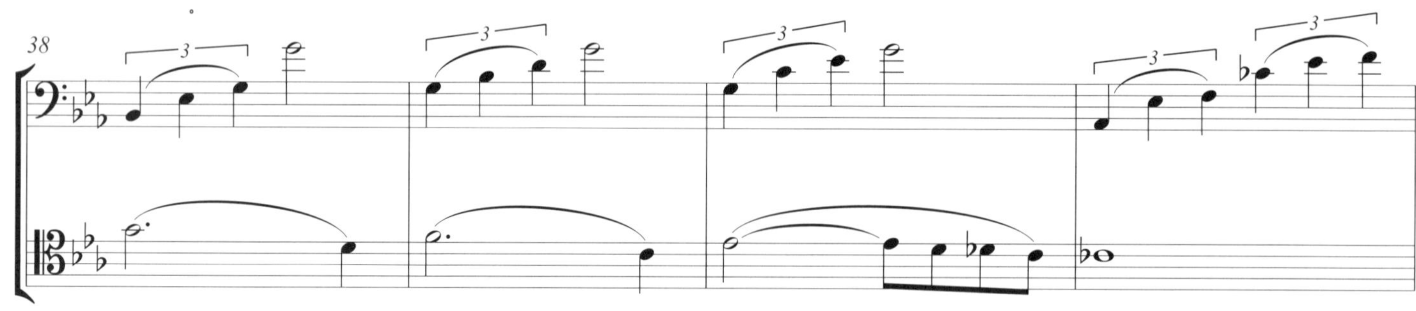
38

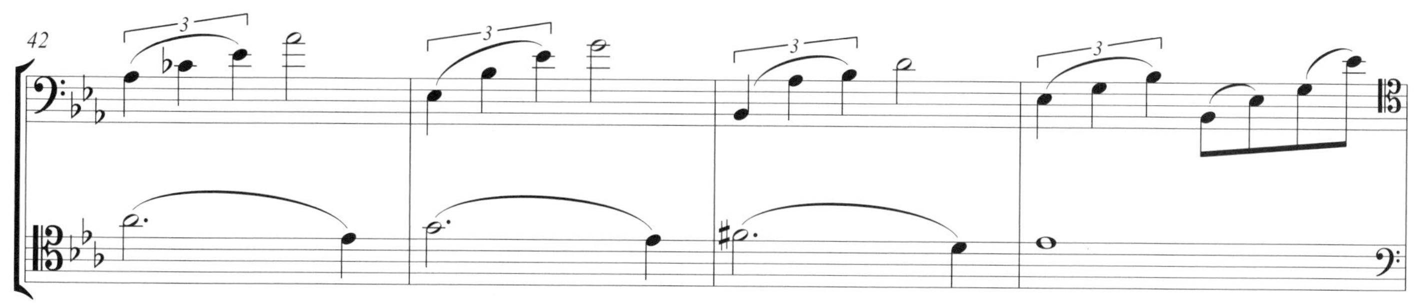
42
3
3
3
3

46
f
3
3
3
3
3

50
3
3

54
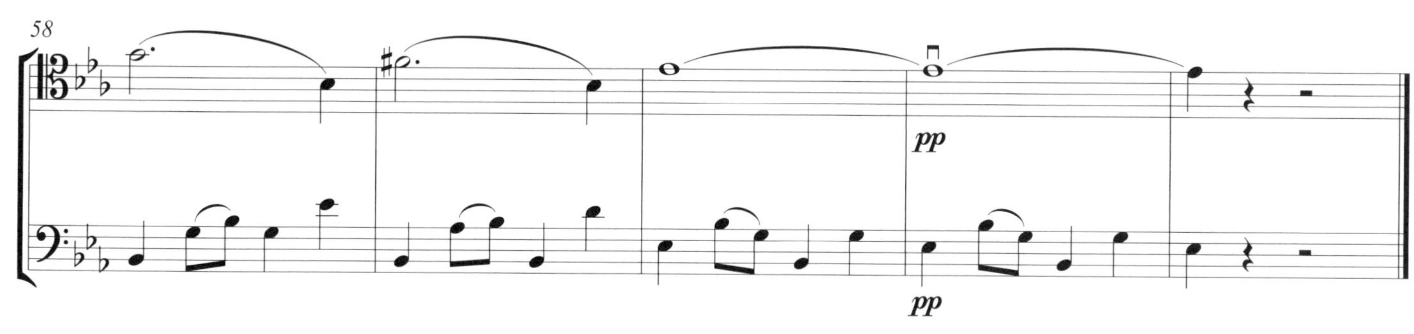
58
pp
pp

Cinema Paradiso

from CINEMA PARADISO

By Ennio Morricone and Andrea Morricone

Arranged by Massimiliano Martinelli and Fulvia Mancini

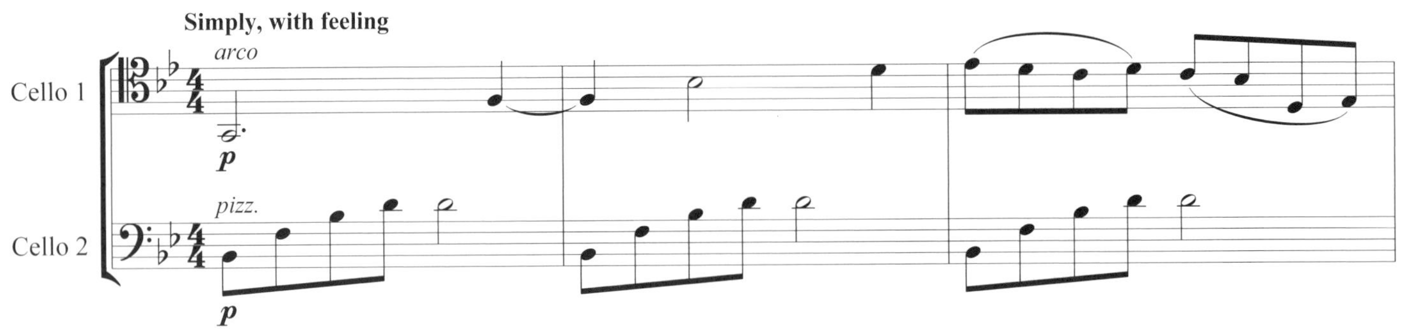

13
f
mf

17

21

24
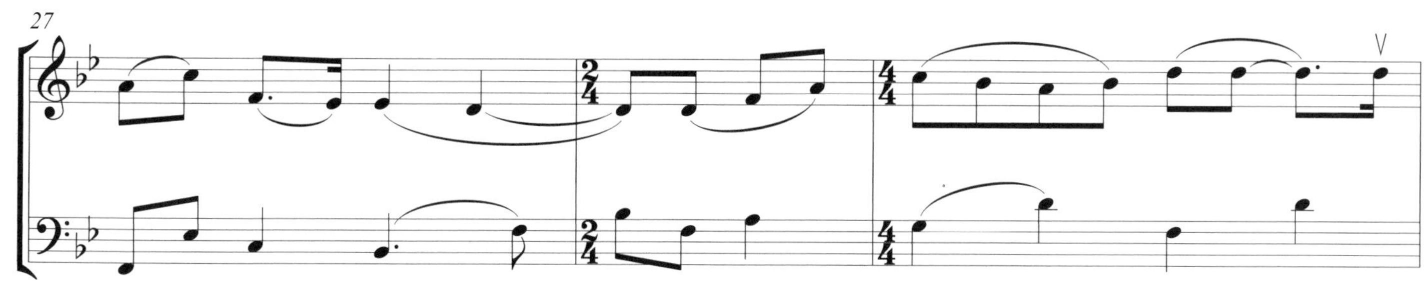
27

30

33
mf
f

37

41
dim.
dim.

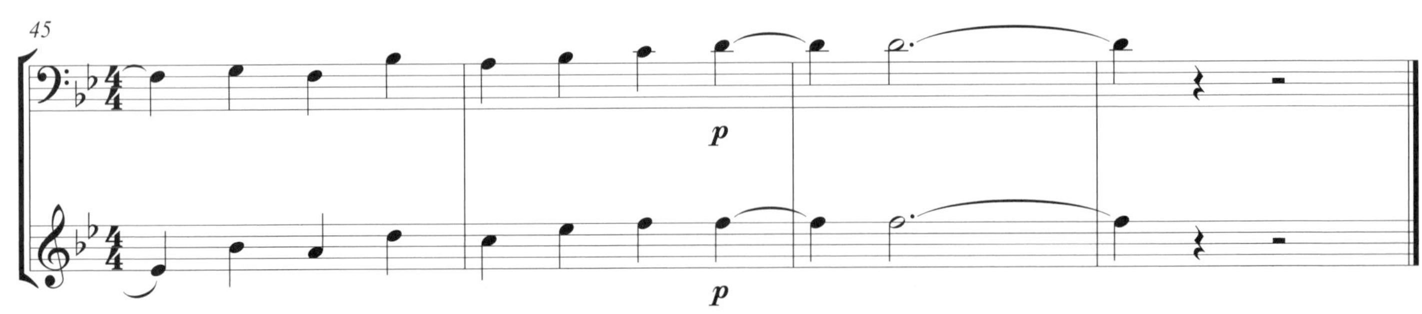
45
p
p

Eye of the Tiger

Theme from ROCKY III

Words and Music by Frank Sullivan and Jim Peterik
Arranged by Massimiliano Martinelli and Fulvia Mancini

10
3

13

16

19
3

22
ff
ff

25

28
3
3

31
1.
2.

Deborah's Theme

from ONCE UPON A TIME IN AMERICA

By Ennio Morricone

Arranged by Massimiliano Martinelli and Fulvia Mancini

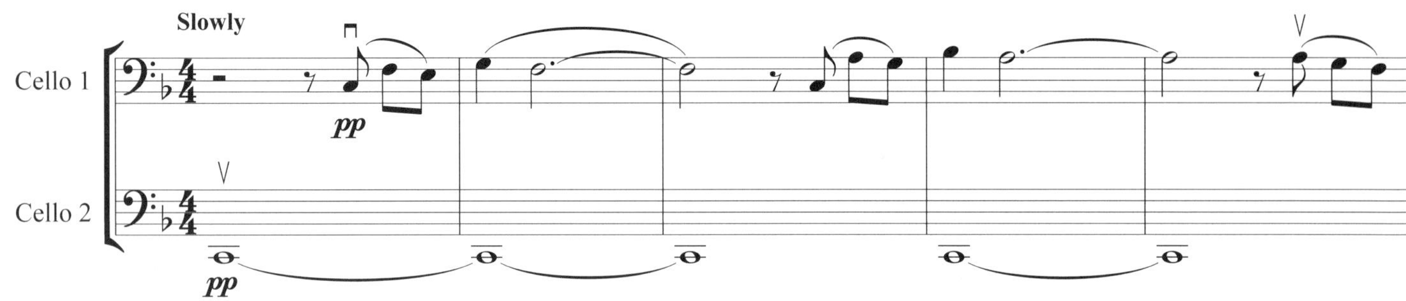

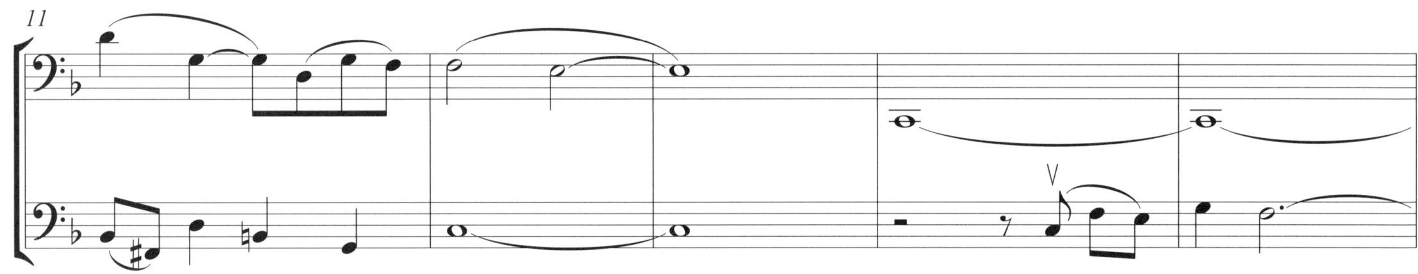

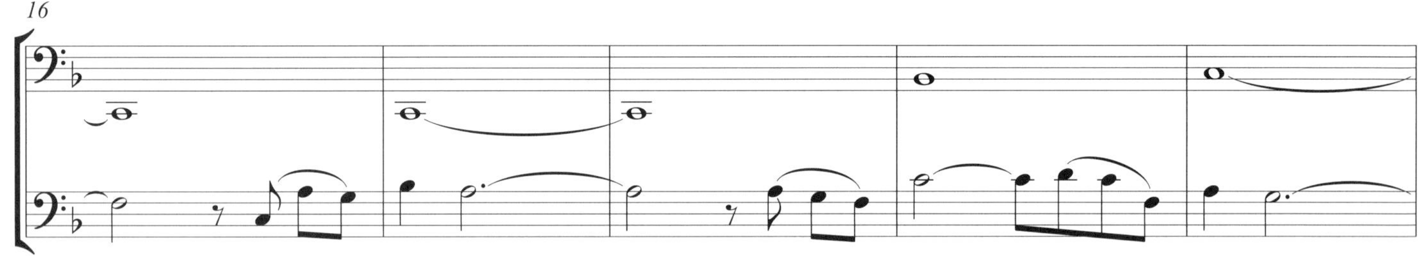

26
31
mf
mf
cresc.
cresc.
35
f
f
ff
ff
40
dim.
dim.
pp
p
45
50

Godfather Medley

from the Paramount Pictures films THE GODFATHER and THE GODFATHER PART II

By Nino Rota
Arranged by Massimiliano Martinelli and Fulvia Mancini

Godfather Finale
from the Paramount Pictures film THE GODFATHER

Expressively

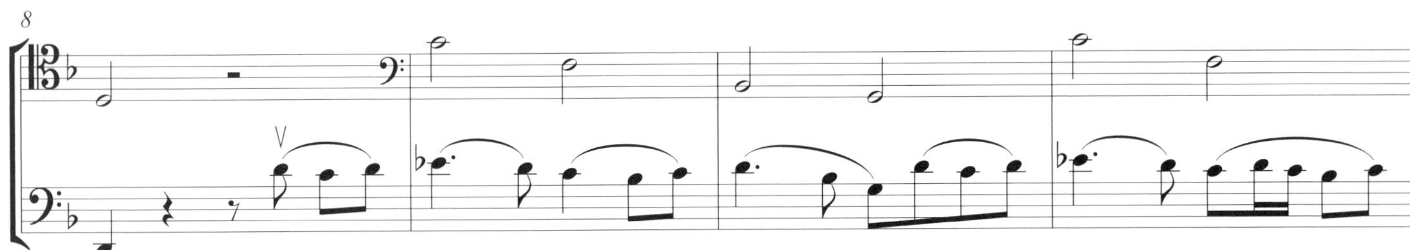

The Immigrant
from the Paramount Pictures film THE GODFATHER PART II

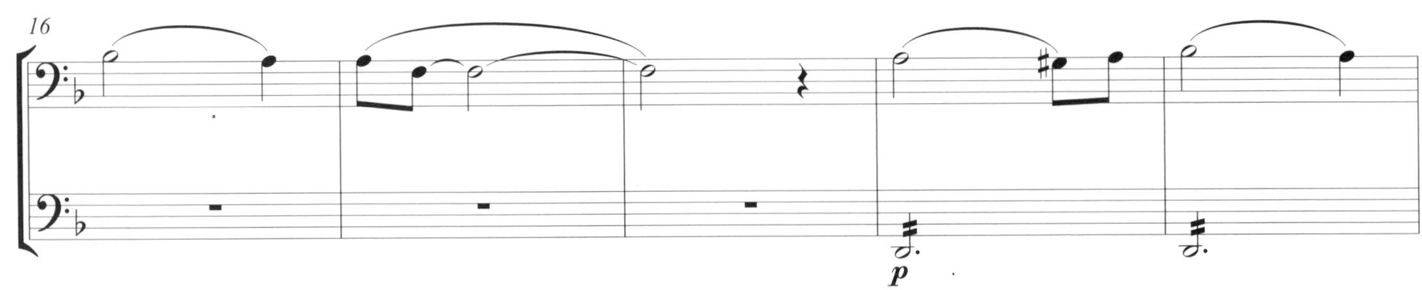

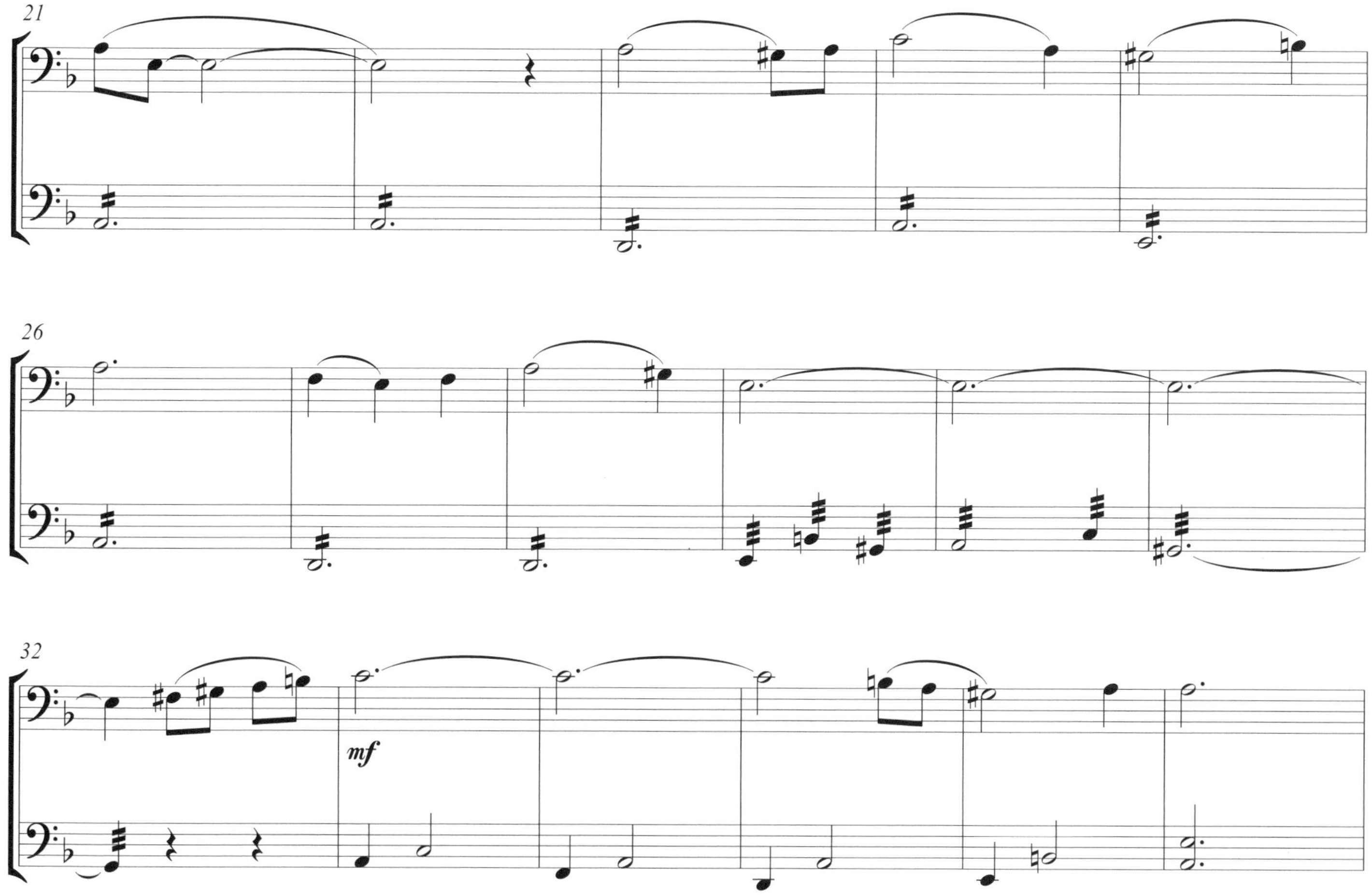

21

26

32

mf

38

f

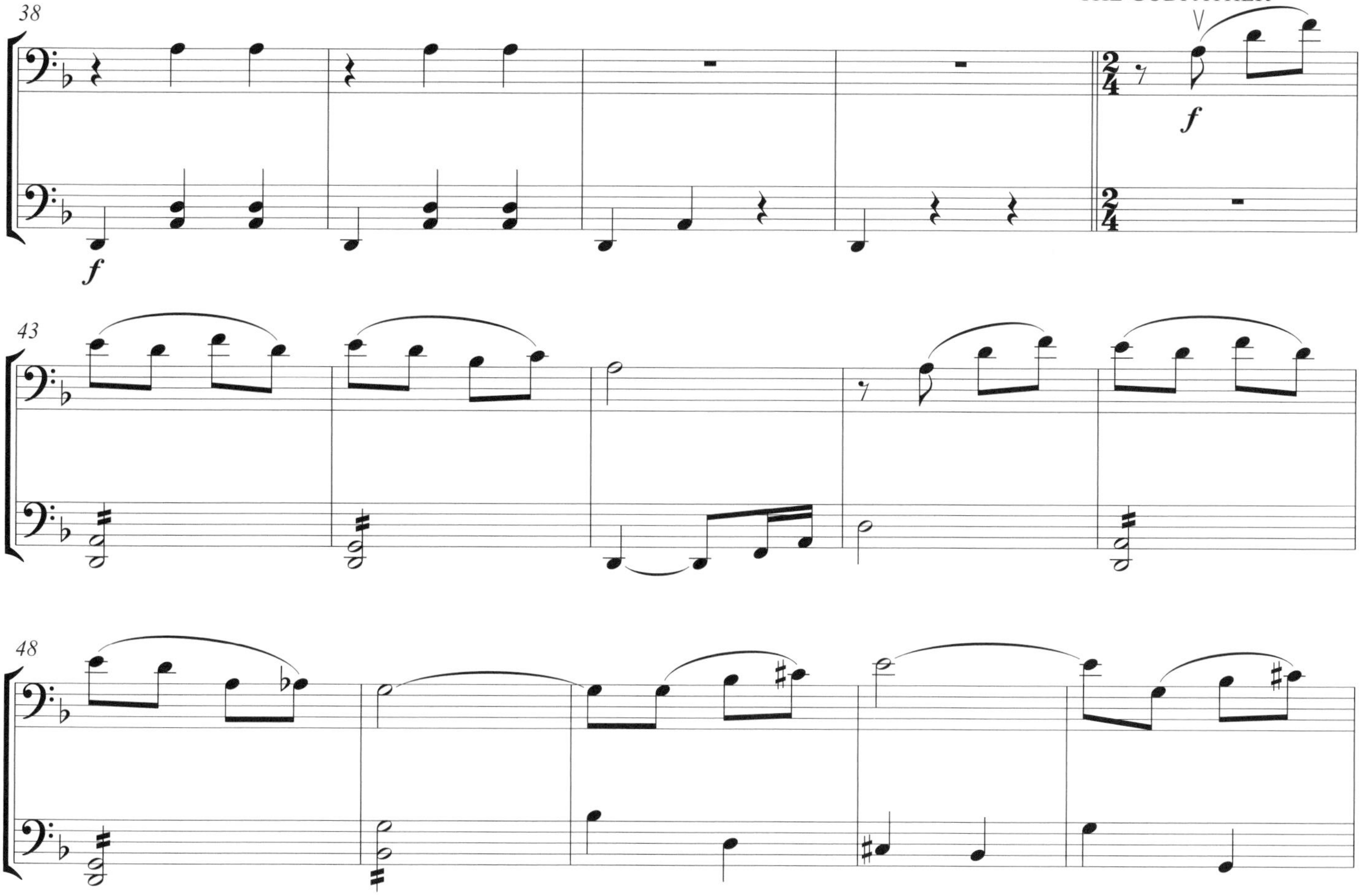

The Godfather (Love Theme)
from the Paramount Pictures film
THE GODFATHER

f

43

48

53
58
63
68
73
78

CELLO 1

GREAT MOVIE THEMES

FOR CELLO DUET

arranged by Mr & Mrs Cello

ISBN 978-1-70515-703-9

Visit Hal Leonard Online at
www.halleonard.com

World headquarters, contact:
Hal Leonard
7777 West Bluemound Road
Milwaukee, WI 53213
Email: info@halleonard.com

In Europe, contact:
Hal Leonard Europe Limited
42 Wigmore Street
Marylebone, London, W1U 2RY
Email: info@halleonardeurope.com

In Australia, contact:
Hal Leonard Australia Pty. Ltd.
4 Lentara Court
Cheltenham, Victoria, 3192 Australia
Email: info@halleonard.com.au

Amarcord

Theme from the film AMARCORD

By Nino Rota

Arranged by Massimiliano Martinelli and Fulvia Mancini

Cinema Paradiso

from CINEMA PARADISO
By Ennio Morricone and Andrea Morricone
Arranged by Massimiliano Martinelli and Fulvia Mancini

Deborah's Theme

from ONCE UPON A TIME IN AMERICA
By Ennio Morricone
Arranged by Massimiliano Martinelli and Fulvia Mancini

Cello 1

Eye of the Tiger

Theme from ROCKY III

Words and Music by Frank Sullivan and Jim Peterik

Arranged by Massimiliano Martinelli and Fulvia Mancini

Godfather Medley

from the Paramount Pictures films THE GODFATHER and THE GODFATHER PART II
By Nino Rota
Arranged by Massimiliano Martinelli and Fulvia Mancini

from the Paramount Pictures film THE GODFATHER

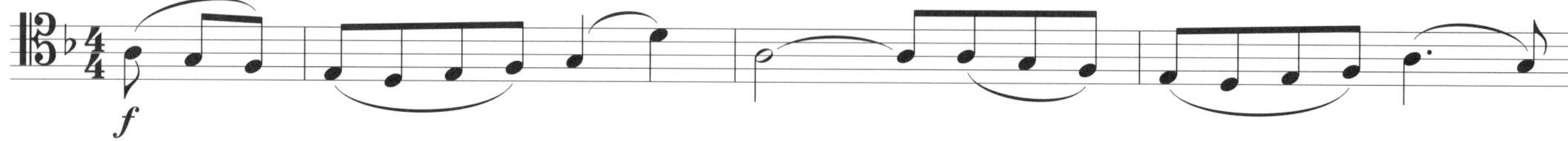

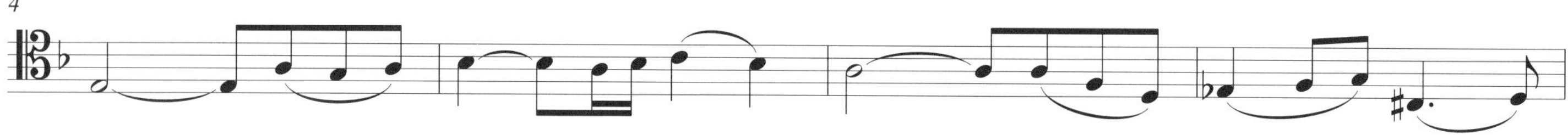

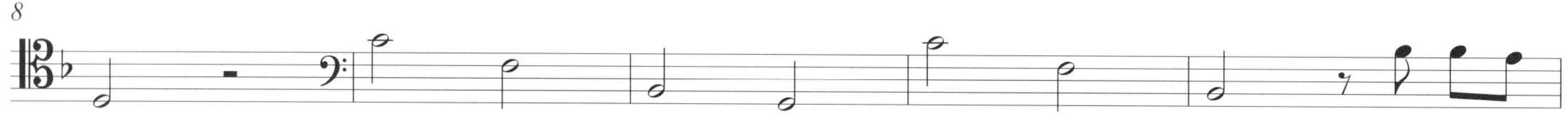

The Immigrant
from the Paramount Pictures film THE GODFATHER PART II

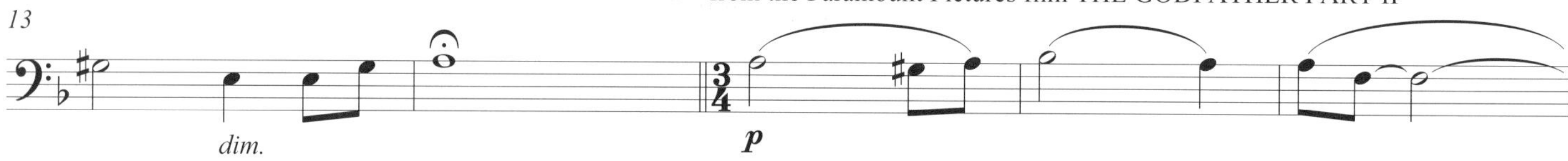

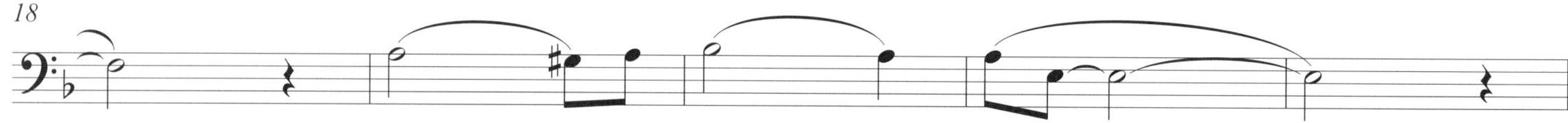

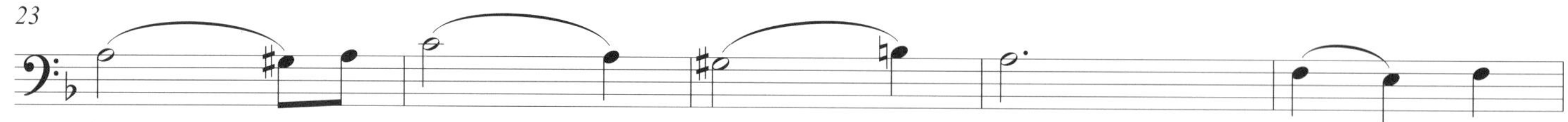

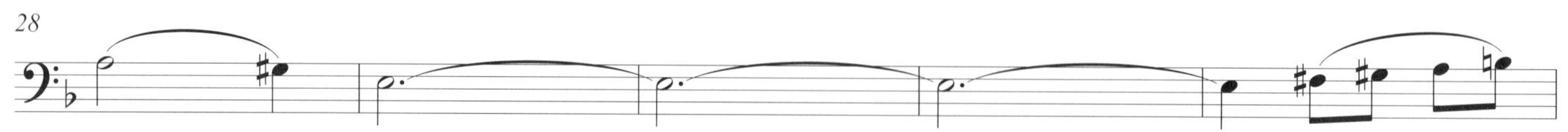

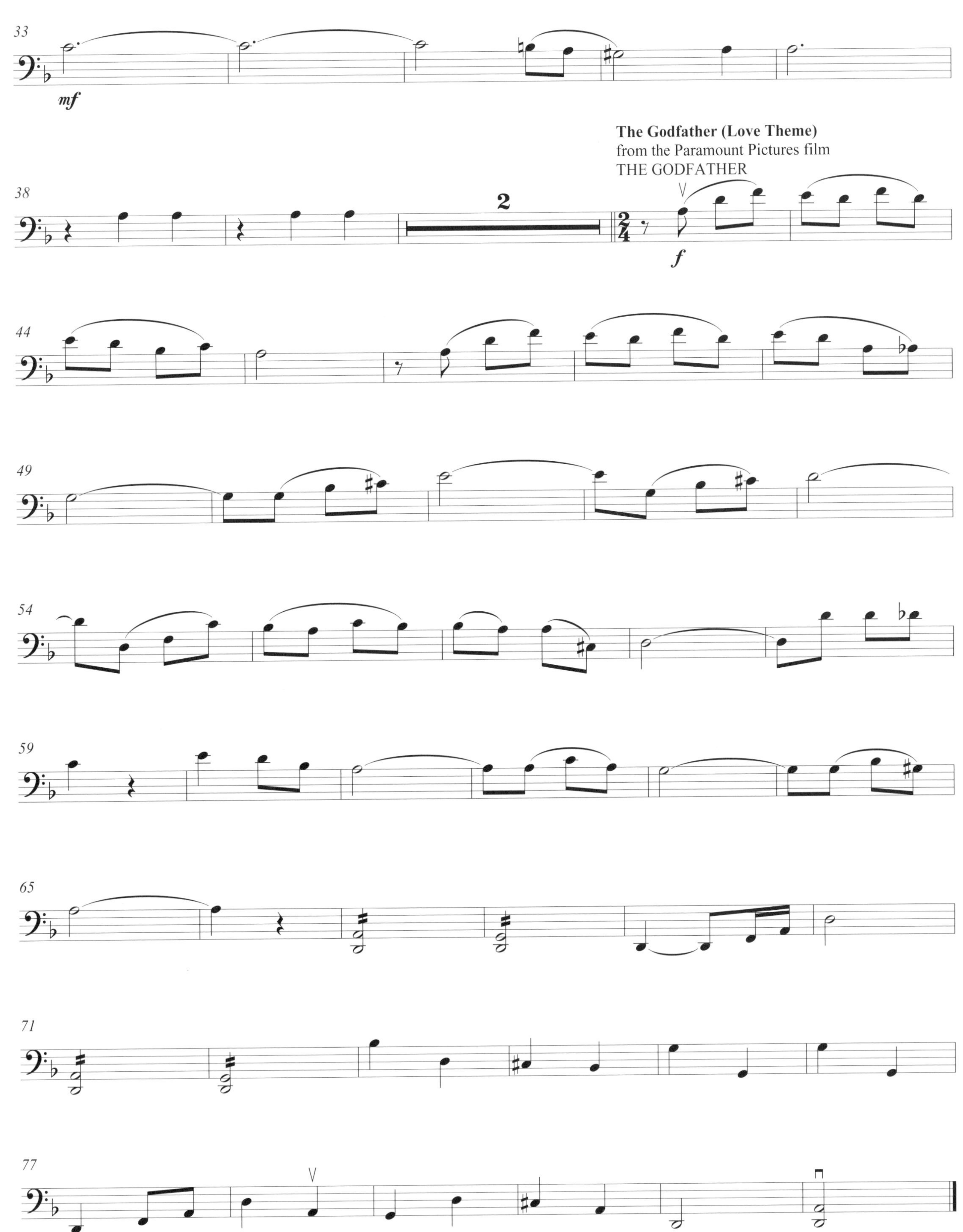
33
mf
The Godfather (Love Theme)
from the Paramount Pictures film
THE GODFATHER
38
2
f
44
49
54
59
65
71
77

Love Story

Theme from the Paramount Picture LOVE STORY
Music by Francis Lai
Arranged by Massimiliano Martinelli and Fulvia Mancini

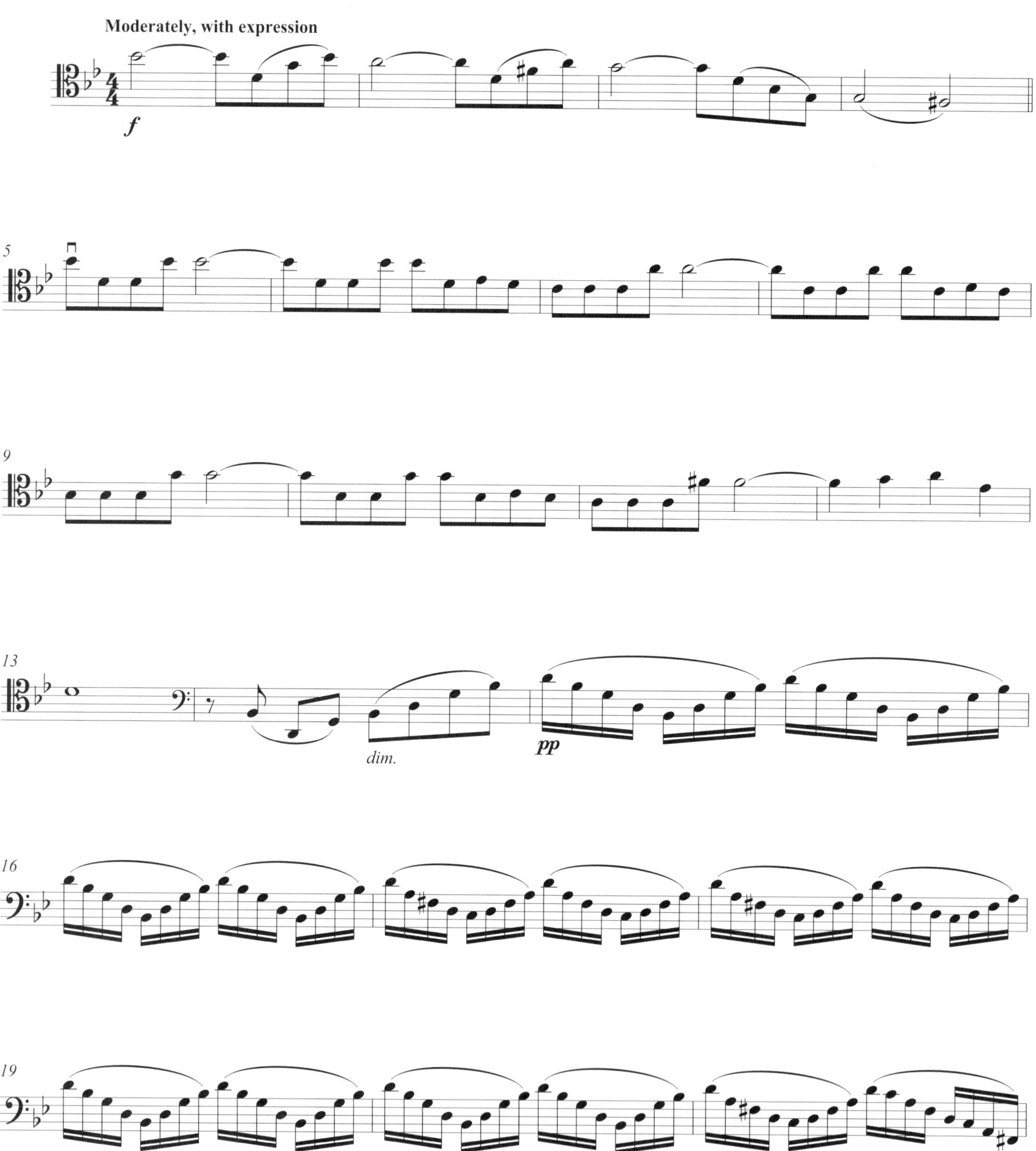

22
cresc.
f

26

30

34
3
dim.
rit.

38
a tempo
3
3

42
3

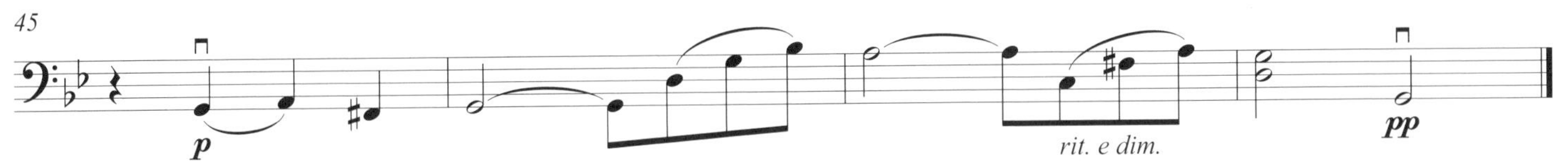
45
p
rit. e dim.
pp

Mia & Sebastian's Theme

from LA LA LAND
Music by Justin Hurwitz
Arranged by Massimiliano Martinelli and Fulvia Mancini

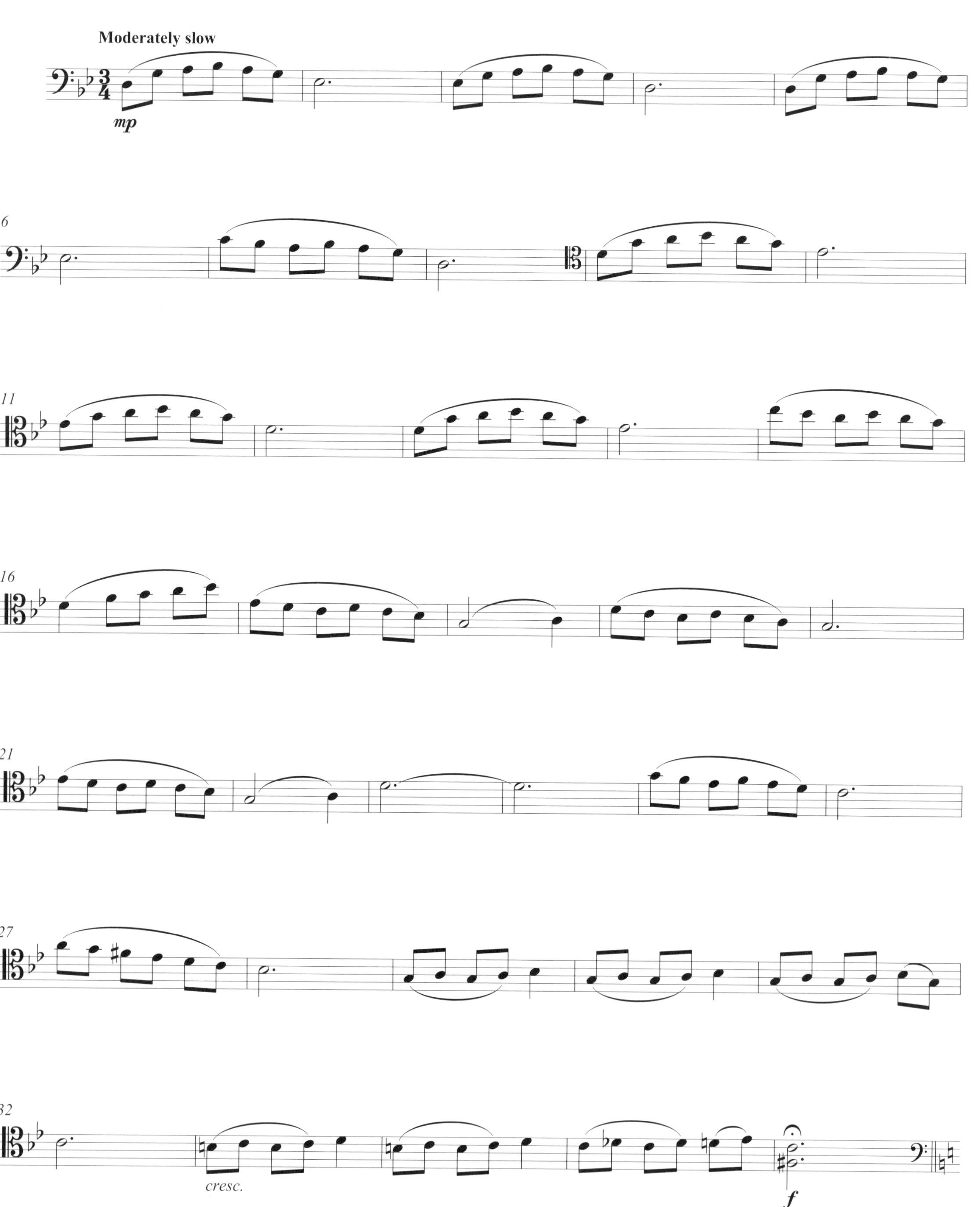

37
mp
42
47
52
57
61
66
cresc.
71
p
76

Cello 1

Mission: Impossible Theme

from the Paramount Motion Picture MISSION: IMPOSSIBLE
By Lalo Schifrin
Arranged by Massimiliano Martinelli and Fulvia Mancini

24
27
30
33
36
p
38
40
42
44
ff

Cello 1

No Time to Die

from NO TIME TO DIE

Words and Music by Billie Eilish O'Connell and Finneas O'Connell
Arranged by Massimiliano Martinelli and Fulvia Mancini

33
dim.
37
mp
41
44
47
mf
50
53
dim.
mf
3
57
cresc.
f
61
p
64

Moon River

from the Paramount Picture BREAKFAST AT TIFFANY'S
Words by Johnny Mercer
Music by Henry Mancini
Arranged by Massimiliano Martinelli and Fulvia Mancini

CELLO 2

GREAT MOVIE THEMES

FOR CELLO DUET

arranged by Mr & Mrs Cello

ISBN 978-1-70515-703-9

Visit Hal Leonard Online at
www.halleonard.com

World headquarters, contact:
Hal Leonard
7777 West Bluemound Road
Milwaukee, WI 53213
Email: info@halleonard.com

In Europe, contact:
Hal Leonard Europe Limited
42 Wigmore Street
Marylebone, London, W1U 2RY
Email: info@halleonardeurope.com

In Australia, contact:
Hal Leonard Australia Pty. Ltd.
4 Lentara Court
Cheltenham, Victoria, 3192 Australia
Email: info@halleonard.com.au

00391742

Amarcord

Theme from the film AMARCORD
By Nino Rota
Arranged by Massimiliano Martinelli and Fulvia Mancini

Cello 2

Cinema Paradiso

from CINEMA PARADISO
By Ennio Morricone and Andrea Morricone
Arranged by Massimiliano Martinelli and Fulvia Mancini

Deborah's Theme

from ONCE UPON A TIME IN AMERICA

By Ennio Morricone

Arranged by Massimiliano Martinelli and Fulvia Mancini

Cello 2

Eye of the Tiger

Theme from ROCKY III

Words and Music by Frank Sullivan and Jim Peterik
Arranged by Massimiliano Martinelli and Fulvia Mancini

Godfather Medley

from the Paramount Pictures films THE GODFATHER and THE GODFATHER PART II
By Nino Rota
Arranged by Massimiliano Martinelli and Fulvia Mancini

The Godfather (Love Theme)
from the Paramount Pictures film THE GODFATHER

Love Story

Theme from the Paramount Picture LOVE STORY
Music by Francis Lai
Arranged by Massimiliano Martinelli and Fulvia Mancini

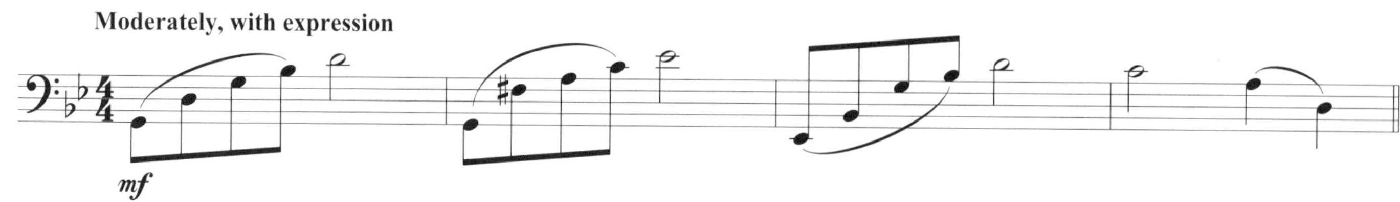

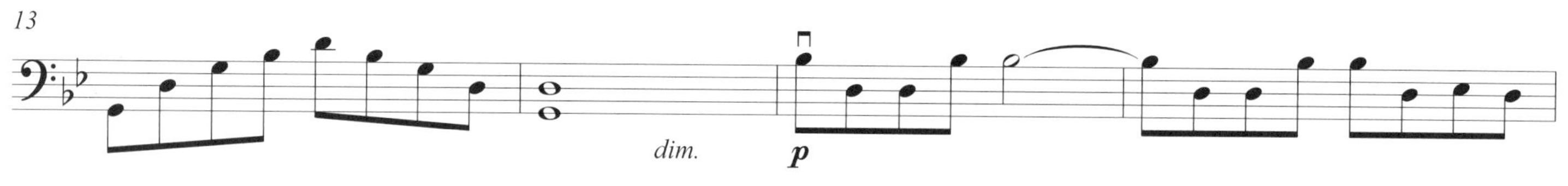

25
f
28
31
34
dim.
rit.
38
a tempo
42
45
rit. e dim.
pp

Cello 2

Mia & Sebastian's Theme

from LA LA LAND

Music by Justin Hurwitz

Arranged by Massimiliano Martinelli and Fulvia Mancini

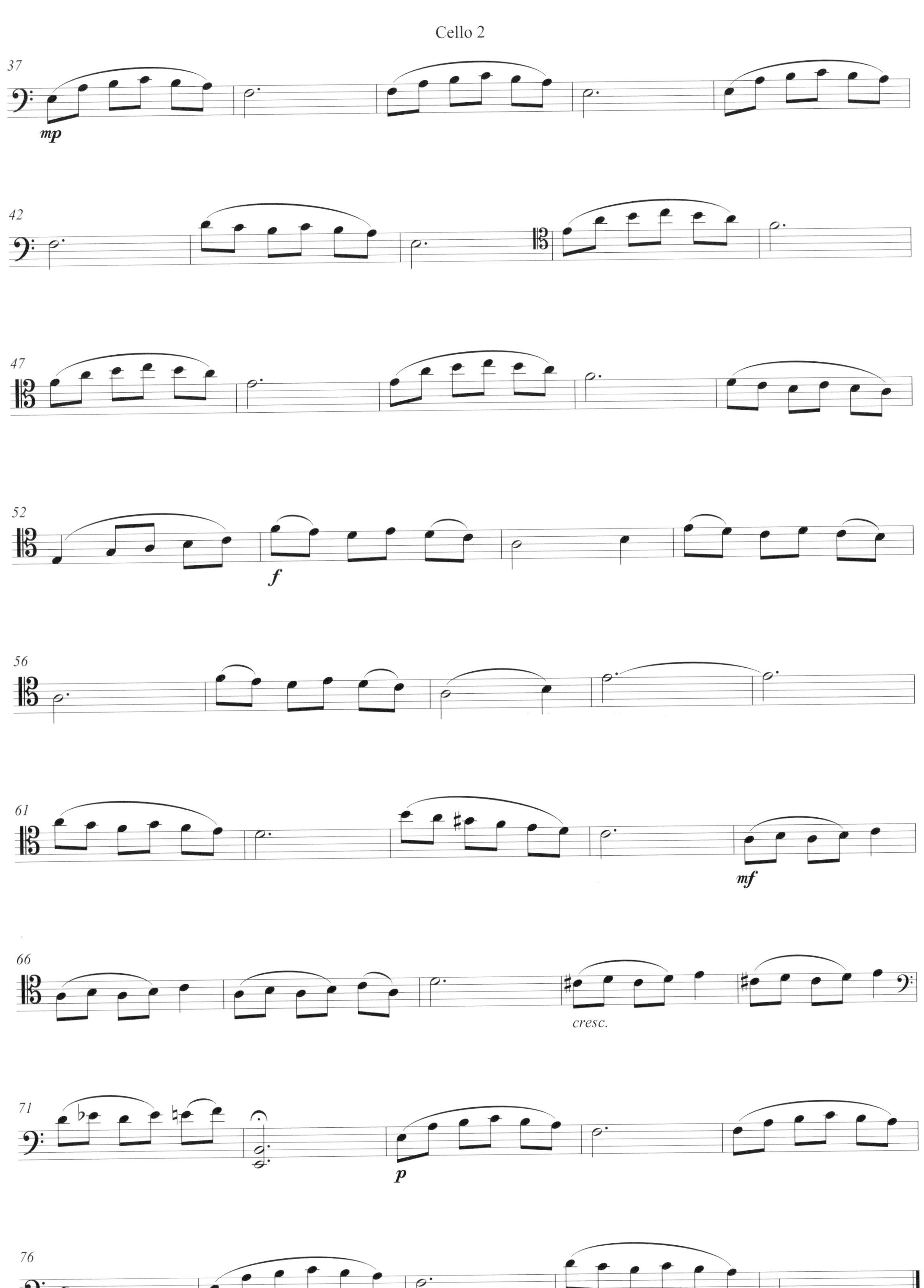
37
mp
42
47
52
f
56
61
mf
66
cresc.
71
p
76

Cello 2

Mission: Impossible Theme

from the Paramount Motion Picture MISSION: IMPOSSIBLE
By Lalo Schifrin
Arranged by Massimiliano Martinelli and Fulvia Mancini

22
25
28
31
34
37
p
41
44
ff

No Time to Die

from NO TIME TO DIE

Words and Music by Billie Eilish O'Connell and Finneas O'Connell
Arranged by Massimiliano Martinelli and Fulvia Mancini

32
f
35
dim.
p
39
43
47
mf
51
dim.
55
mf
cresc.
f
59
p
63

Moon River

from the Paramount Picture BREAKFAST AT TIFFANY'S
Words by Johnny Mercer
Music by Henry Mancini
Arranged by Massimiliano Martinelli and Fulvia Mancini

Love Story

Theme from the Paramount Picture LOVE STORY

Music by Francis Lai

Arranged by Massimiliano Martinelli and Fulvia Mancini

13
dim.
dim.
pp
p
16
19
22
cresc.
cresc.
25
f
f
28

31
34
dim.
dim.
37
rit.
rit.
a tempo
a tempo
40
43
p
46
rit. e dim.
rit. e dim.
pp
pp

Mia & Sebastian's Theme

from LA LA LAND

Music by Justin Hurwitz

Arranged by Massimiliano Martinelli and Fulvia Mancini

21
26
31
cresc.
cresc.
36
f
f
mp
mp
41
46

51
f
56
61
mf
66
cresc.
cresc.
71
p
p
76

Mission: Impossible Theme

from the Paramount Motion Picture MISSION: IMPOSSIBLE

By Lalo Schifrin

Arranged by Massimiliano Martinelli and Fulvia Mancini

16
arco
19
22
25
28
31

34
3
3
36
p
p
38
40
42
44
ff
ff

No Time to Die

from NO TIME TO DIE

Words and Music by Billie Eilish O'Connell and Finneas O'Connell

Arranged by Massimiliano Martinelli and Fulvia Mancini

13
16
pp
p
19
22
mp
25
28
mf
mf

31
f
34
dim.
dim.
37
mp
p
40
43
46
mf
mf

49
52
dim.
dim.
55
mf
mf
3
cresc.
cresc.
58
f
f
61
p
p
64

Moon River

from the Paramount Picture BREAKFAST AT TIFFANY'S

Words by Johnny Mercer
Music by Henry Mancini
Arranged by Massimiliano Martinelli and Fulvia Mancini

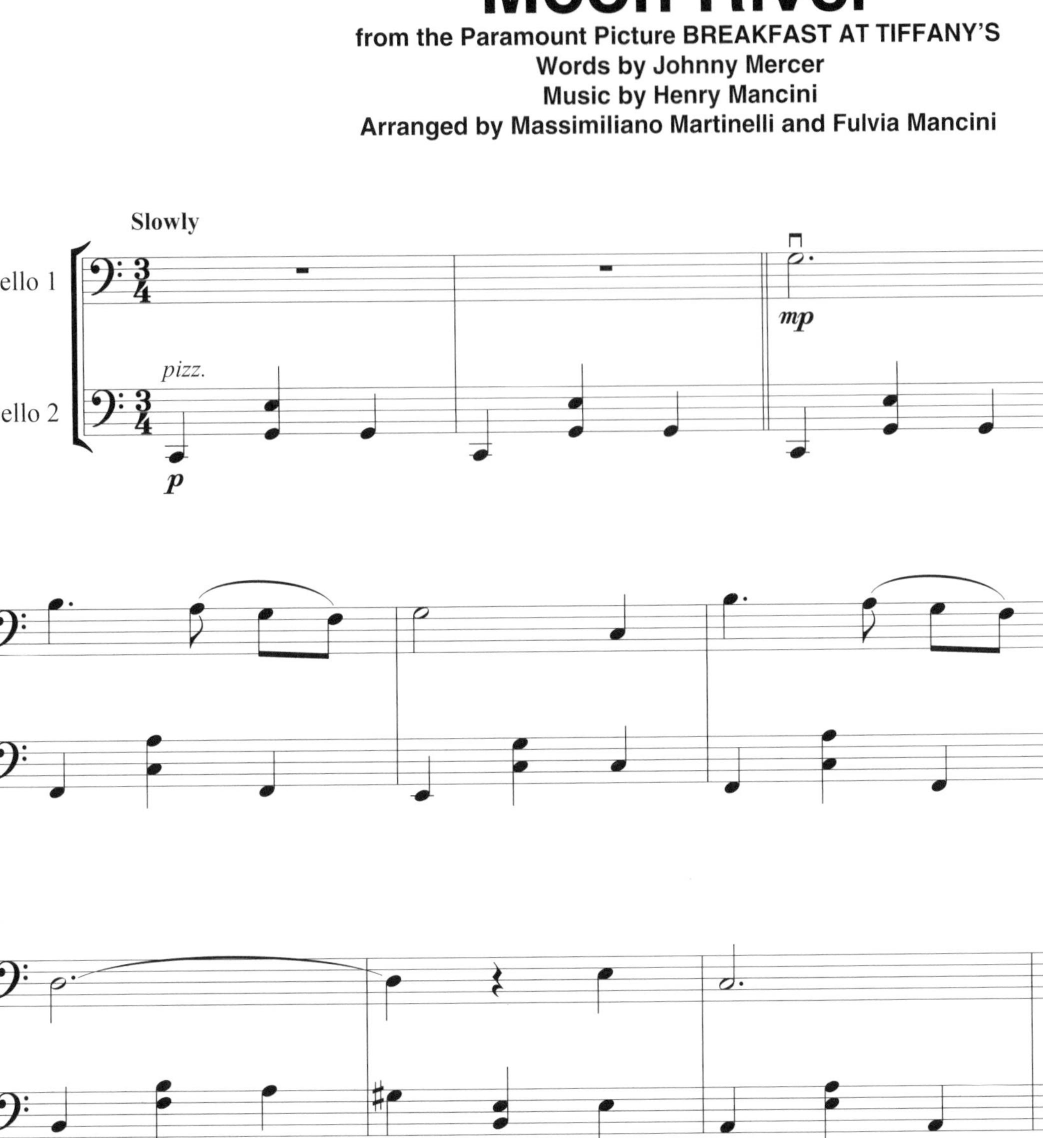

21
25
30
34
38
f

42
46
50
54
58